MY FRIEND NICKY

DOG STORY

KRITIKA SAPRA

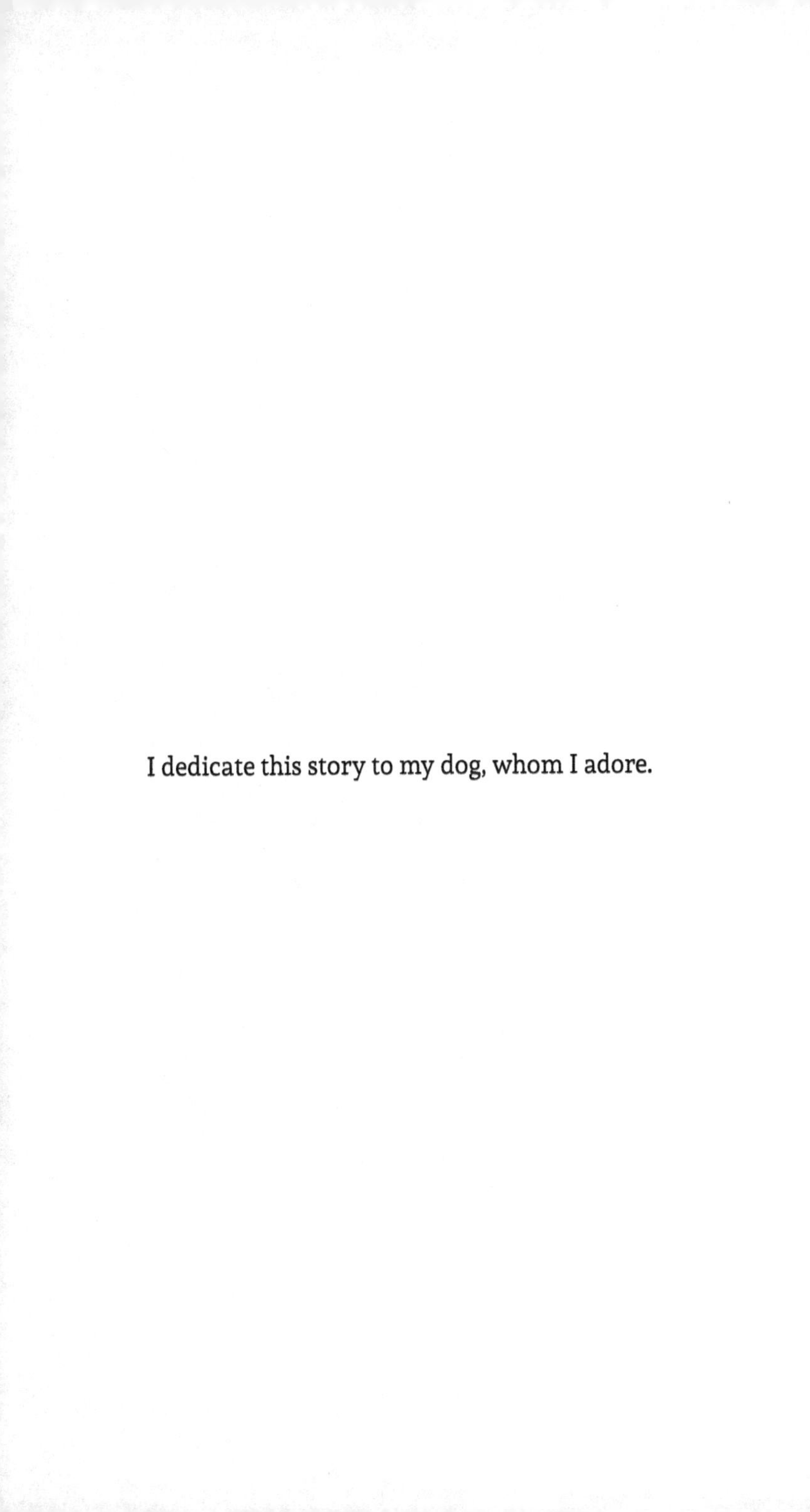
I dedicate this story to my dog, whom I adore.

Contents

Foreword

I'd want to thank my puppy for its affection for our family.I have a strong bond to my dog, and I am sharing his journey with you all. I hope you like this story.

Acknowledgements

I would like to express my deepest gratitude to my loving pet, whose presence filled our lives with joy, loyalty, and unforgettable moments. This story is a true reflection of our journey together, and all the characters mentioned are real, sharing a bond that goes beyond words.

To my family, thank you for your love and support throughout this journey, especially my father, whose love for my pet will always remain cherished in my heart.

Lastly, to all the pet lovers out there who understand the profound connection we share with our animals—this story is for you. May it bring comfort, love, and a reminder that pets are family, and their love is eternal.

ACKNOWLEDGEMENTS

Kritika Sapra Books Written -Vengeanv
ce,Vengeance1,Terror,Anew beginning,Losses as
Lessons,Letter from Heaven, Boy with big eyes and many
more .

ACKNOWLEDGEMENTS

1

A Dog's Diary

My First Day

I remember when I was hidden in a basket. I was so scared; I was only around 15 days old when my mother and I were separated. They took me away from her. I could see my brother and sister—everyone was being separated. That was the last time I drank my mother's milk. I saw a few faces that took me and put me in a cage where I could see other dogs. In the cage above me, there were cats, pigeons, kittens, and more puppies, all separated from their parents. I felt terrified. I never imagined this could happen, especially after enjoying the warmth and cuddles from my mom. I remembered every moment I had shared with her as I sat down in the corner, trembling.

They placed us in a large van. It seemed like they were going to kill us all, and I was petrified. I sat in the corner of my cage, looking out the window with sadness, knowing deep down that I would never see my mom again. After some time, I fell asleep. I woke up a few hours later to loud noises and shouting. They were grabbing the puppies by their tails. Were they going to hurt us? I was terrified.

They took our cage out and placed us, one by one, into a storage room filled with animals, including birds and fishes. They offered us water and milk. I was thirsty, so I hesitantly approached the bowl and, in one gulp, finished all the water. But I was still sorrowful and couldn't eat for a day.

The next day, they moved us into a large cage where all the white dogs were kept together. They then placed us in a shop, on display, awaiting an uncertain future.

Well, I forgot to introduce myself—my name is Niky, and this story is about me. I'm a white Spitz. I'm not sure why they call me a Spitz and not a Pomeranian, but that's what they say. I'm beautiful, smart, intelligent, and sometimes a bit naughty. Now, let's dive into my journey—I promise that by the end, you'll fall in love with my story and feel a deep connection to me. If you're a dog lover, you've definitely chosen the right book!

"*Keywords*

- *Trembling- Shaking slightly because of fear, cold, or nervousness.*
- *Terrified -Very scared or frightened.*
- *Uncertain-Not sure about what will happen in the future; unpredictable.*
- *Gulp -To swallow something quickly or in large amounts.*
- *Display- To show something for others to view*

"

2

From Cage to Home

The next day, they sent me to another shop. This shop had fewer animals—only dogs, puppies, and cats. In my cage, there was a friendly white dog, but he had less fur than me, and his white coat was a bit pale. I thought I looked smarter than him. He rested his head on mine and fell asleep—oh, he was heavy! I barked at him in my sweet little voice, which made the people outside laugh. A few of them came over to see me, but they seemed to find the other dog cuter than me. They took him out, cuddled him, held him in their arms, and took him away from me.

They had categorized us. They called him a Labra. I watched as a lady took him, paid with a few pieces of paper—they called them rupees. I overheard them talking in a language that was difficult for me to understand. I only knew two gestures: anger and love, nothing else.

Then, a black dog that looked similar to me came over and tugged on my ear. I barked again, and this time, a boy noticed me. He picked me up and said something I couldn't quite understand at first, but I soon realized he was planning to gift me to his girlfriend.

Finally, someone took me. I was free from that jail. He bought a basket for me, and I felt a little scared at first. He brought me to his home, a place without a big cage. There were a few people there who seemed a bit scared of me, and, on the other hand, I was scared of them. I was trying to find a place where I could hide. The boy was nice—he gave me plenty of food. Finally, I fell asleep in the corner of a chair.

The next day, he put me in the basket and left. I looked back at the house, my eyes lingering on the gate, and I felt scared again. I had grown attached to that boy; he was very kind. But I couldn't help but wonder if he was going to sell me. After some time, I saw a pretty girl. The boy handed her my basket, and she looked happy. I felt happy too, but I was still scared because I never fully trusted humans. I had gotten attached to my mom, but she was taken from me. Then, I got attached to this boy, and he handed me over to this girl. I was worried that if I got attached to her, she might give me to someone else. I was very scared. They talked for a while, and after that,she took me to her home.

3

Tears and Prayers

I don't know why she was hiding me, but I wanted freedom. At night, she arranged a chair for me and made a comfortable bed. She kept her chair next to mine, but I got up—I wasn't comfortable, and I wanted to leave that home. Maybe I was missing my mom; I needed her milk and love. I was also missing my brother. I got down from the chair and hid under the fridge. In the morning, she and her sister were looking for me, but they didn't tell their dad that they had a puppy. Finally, they found me sleeping under the fridge tray. I was cold and shivering. They took me out and gave me some warm milk.

One night, while I was roaming around the room, their father caught me. I was caught red-handed! I didn't know what they were talking about, so I quietly went to the kitchen, where I had hidden my milky bone. I took it out and ate it, and they all laughed. That day finally ended, and I felt that everything was balanced.

A few days later, I became ill. I pooped a lot and vomited. The girl was scared and cried a lot, day and night. I remember her taking me to the hospital, crying because she knew I was going to die. But I was praying to God to make me fit because her soul was pure. A few hours later, I saw the same boy who had handed me to her. They both took me to a place where other dogs were crying as they were being given needles. Seeing this, I trembled with fear. But I wasn't fully conscious—I had become weak since I hadn't eaten anything for the past two days. The doctor was talking about something called parvovirus. I don't know exactly what it is, but it's some kind of virus that affects puppies. They said I was infected before he purchased me. The girl cried, but they gave me an injection, and after some time, I felt hungry. I asked her for something to eat. She gave me food, hugged me, and thanked God.

Her name is Kritika, and you all know her. She is the author of *Vengeance*, *Terror*, *Losses as Lessons*, and many more, and now she's writing about me.

4

From Cuddles to Checkups

After a few days, I became friendly. My favorite toys were teddy bears, and I loved the game where someone would throw a ball or bottle for me to catch and play with.

They often took me to the park, where I would run around, but in the end, I always cuddled with them and fell asleep in their bed. That bed was soft and comfy, and I loved sleeping with them. After some time, I even felt comfortable sleeping with their father. Everything was going well.

I usually went on little "dates" with my sister, where she would tie a rakhi on me during the occasion and bring me gifts and treats. I felt so happy and comfortable. I also loved tearing things apart. When I was 6 months old, there was a female dog named Lucy; she was our neighbor's dog. She used to come to my gate, eager for me to play with her. Seeing her excitement made me want to play with her too. But after a few days, I heard that she had left home. Our neighbors searched for her from morning until night, and my family also went out to look for her. Unfortunately, they lost hope. My sister told me that if I ever did the same, the dogs outside might hurt me.

I promised her that I would never do something like that. A few days later, we were out walking, and I saw Lucy sitting by the roadside. She was hurt and had some bite marks. I barked at her, asking where she had been. She recognized us and followed us, wagging her tail with a sense of satisfaction, knowing she would finally meet her owner again. When she did, they thanked me for finding her.

As I get older, my vision is becoming blurry, but the story I'm sharing captures some of my best moments and my journey.

One day, while I was walking with my sister, I felt an itch in my ear. I was scratching it badly. My sister noticed and took out a dark, warm thing from my ear. What was that? Was it a parasite? I was scared and asked her to wash my feet, but she refused and said, "You need a bath."

A bath? Why do people always say that we need to take a bath to remove any parasite? I didn't want to take a bath. I had heard this word before—I had seen them pour water on themselves and change their clothes. I went along with it, but when they poured water over me, my opinion of humans changed. She put some water and shampoo on me, and I decided that this word, "bath," only means one thing: danger.

Now, whenever she says "bath," I hide under the sofa and growl at her. But she's clever—she knows how to distract me. She says, "Treat! Who wants a treat?" I come out from under the sofa, and she takes me straight to the bathroom. One day, she suddenly came and took me. You should at least tell me where you're taking me! She brought me to the bathroom and poured water on me. I growled at her, but she's a tough lady.

Every year, as I get older, she takes me for checkups twice a year. They give me a few injections and then let me go. I've heard about some dangerous diseases like puppy DP, corona, 9-in-1, deworming, rabies, and many more. She used to give me a deworming tablet that the doctor told her to hide in something sweet, like a rasgulla. But I'm smart enough—I ate the rasgulla and left the tablet aside.

5

From Leashes to Love: My Journey with Kritika

A few years passed, and now I was able to understand a few words like "leash," "walk," "eat," "mouse," "cat," and "treat." I knew these words made me happy, even though, at first, it was tough to understand why they were using such words. Now I understood—it wasn't that difficult after all.

I had become an adopted child in the family. Whenever my sister, Kritika, told me to get my leash, I would search with my wide nose, sniffing around until I found it. I knew that word meant a trip to the park, where I could see the greenery, meet other dogs, and bark at them to have a little chat or play. Some dogs barked back, and some came closer, wagging their tails. I spent my days walking and tugging on my leash, trying to tell her that I wanted to chase them.

I remember one time when she was sitting with her friends, and I suddenly spotted squirrels and birds—I chased them! It was so much fun. Kritika always gave me my favorite dishes: curd rice, chapati with milk, dog food, and treats. She is such a humble person, and I love her a lot.

But I also learned a few "dangerous" words like "bath." That word meant she was going to pour water on me. Why would she? I thought I was usually cleaner than any person, and dust was something I loved! Whenever she said, "Let's take a bath," I would get chills down my spine and hide under the sofa, warning her not to take me, or I might bite (though I never really would). But she was clever—she always found a way to trick me. When I hid under the sofa, she would say, "Let's go for a walk," and I'd fall into the trap.

She would clean me with fragrant soap, but I never liked it. When I came back inside, I'd see the bedsheet on the ground, so I'd roll around on it, making sure to drain all the water from my fur. Afterward, she would prepare some warm milk for me, which I loved. Daddy also loved me a lot, and I remember him fondly to this day. I don't know where he is now, but I miss him.

There were some other horrible words I learned during my training: "clinic," "doctor," and of course, "bath."

Do you know what my favorite game was? A bottle—an empty bottle that they would throw, and I'd fetch it and bring it back to her. Now, I was about to become an adult, and all the hormones in me were developing. I needed to release them, but I didn't understand why they found it inappropriate.

6

A Bond Beyond Words: My Time with Daddy

Nicky was 20 days old

Daddy was a superb man. He adored me like his own child. He always asked his children about my meals. He played with me when he came back home after work, and I enjoyed being with him. I remember there were three sisters. The eldest one got married before I arrived, so I don't know much about her. I only remember that whenever she visited, they took me to another room because she was scared of me.

You tell me—do I look scary? I never barked, never bit anyone. Well, I understood, and after a while, I allowed myself to go or sit quietly whenever she came over. She even started patting me from a distance. I understood—it happens.

The other two sisters adored me. After they got married, Dad took really good care of me. When Mom prepared food, he would feed me with his hand because I liked it when Dad made little balls of chapati for me. Sometimes, he gave me eggs to help with my protein deficiency. He ate papaya and watermelon, and I would eat them with him. I slept with him, and most of the time we spent together was amazing.

How can I put this into words? It's an expression, but I know you people understand the bond between us. After a few years, I noticed my sister was taking him somewhere. Dad was becoming older and weaker, and I wanted to ask what was happening. I used to lie on his stomach, but this time when I did, he shouted in pain. I had never seen him like that before.

My sister took him to the hospital, and I stayed home. This was before her marriage. Dad was suffering from TB, and it upset me to see the environment at home. But he recovered and promised them he would quit smoking, which he did. However, after my sister's marriage, the same situation occurred again. This time, I noticed everyone was coming to see him.

Why wasn't he able to feed me? Why didn't he want to feed me? I denied the food and asked Dad to feed me, but he was too weak. He tried, but he had difficulty eating. Days passed, and he stayed in one place, sleeping on the sofa. It was a difficult time for me. I wanted him to play, but he just slept.

I understood he wasn't well. He told my sister to take me to her home, and that was the last time I saw my dad. I thought I would be back soon, but it didn't happen. My sister took me to her home, and I saw tears in Dad's eyes. That's when I understood—we were separating forever.

But I will always miss you, Daddy.

7

A Dog's Hope

Miley

Miley was also an adopted child. She was very young when they brought her into their home, and she lived with my sister. She was unique—she had six fingers on both her hands and feet, and her eyes were different, giving her an aggressive look. I remember when my sister first brought her home; she was so small, but she immediately attacked me. I was a reserved kind of dog, so when I saw her, I just warned her, and she listened. Still, she would play and sometimes fight with me, but I ignored it and let her do that.

When she grew up, and I moved to my sister's home due to Dad's worsening condition, things became challenging for me. When I entered, Miley was happy to see me and played with me, but it took me time to adjust. I was comfortable in my old home, and here I felt a little stressed. I even stopped eating, which worried my sister. She tried her best to prepare meals for me, but I couldn't shake the feeling of discomfort, even though I knew some people there loved me. I think this is why Miley started getting offended by me.

Days passed, and I adjusted somewhat, but one day, when I got up to drink water, Miley attacked me. My sister came and held her back, but Miley wouldn't let go. That was the first time I got hurt. Luckily, my sister arrived just in time, and Miley released me. I was safe, but the incident left a deep mark on me, and I wasn't ready to adjust anymore. I wanted to leave this home as soon as possible. After that, my sister kept us separated, but Miley attacked me several more times. Eventually, my sister had to keep me in her room to keep me safe.

It was hard for me. During the afternoons, I would sleep to pass the time, and when my sister arrived, she played with me and made plenty of food. A few months passed, and the attacks became more frequent. This time, my sister decided to send me back home. I was so happy—at least Dad would be there. I was excited to meet Mom and Dad again and share my days spent at my sister's home.

But when I got back, I didn't see Dad. They showed me his picture and cried. I didn't know what was happening—it was just Dad's picture. One part of my eye had developed cataracts as I was getting older, but with my good eye, I could see Dad's photo. I remembered a few days before, Dad had come to me in my dreams and told me how much he missed me. I saw myself hugging him and eating food together. Those memories are with me all the time.

I also remember that before Dad passed away, he came to visit us one night. My sister and I were home, and I barked when he arrived. After that, my sister left, crying. I could understand the feeling, but I still had hope that Dad would be happy when he came back and saw me. I didn't eat the meal Mom had prepared because I wanted to surprise Dad when he got home and cuddle with him. I wanted to tell him how much I had missed him. I sat by the door all night, waiting for Dad, but he never returned.

Eventually, I agreed to eat. Every evening at the same time, I sat by the door, waiting to see if Dad would come. Days passed, and Dad never came back. Whenever I heard a cough or a sound, I would rush to the door, but as time went on, I understood—Dad would never return.

8

15 Years of Loyalty: My Journey with Family

12months

Now, my connection with Mom has become stronger. Mom talks a lot, and I can't always understand who she's talking to or what she's talking about. It's hard to figure out sometimes. I try to talk to her, but I never get a response. Every day, I wake her up and ask her to prepare my meal. She gives me whatever she wants, but she never asks what I actually need.

10 years

Sometimes, I get angry, but she's always in her own world. Still, I'd like to thank her for preparing my meals all the time. She watches videos but makes sure to cook for me as well. Now I know I have to adjust here. Every day starts with my barking—I wake her up for an hour, and then she gives me my dog food. That's how we've been adjusting.

I am 15 years old now. Sometimes I feel like a child, and other times, I'm mature enough to know how to balance things. But now, I'm losing my vision; it's all fading away, and I can only smell the people near me. But I don't regret anything. My life has been full of love, and I thank God for giving me such a life, surrounded by amazing people. I still play with my favorite bottle and enjoy eating potatoes, cucumbers, papayas, and watermelons. I love curry rice and rice with curd, but I also enjoy chapati and milk.

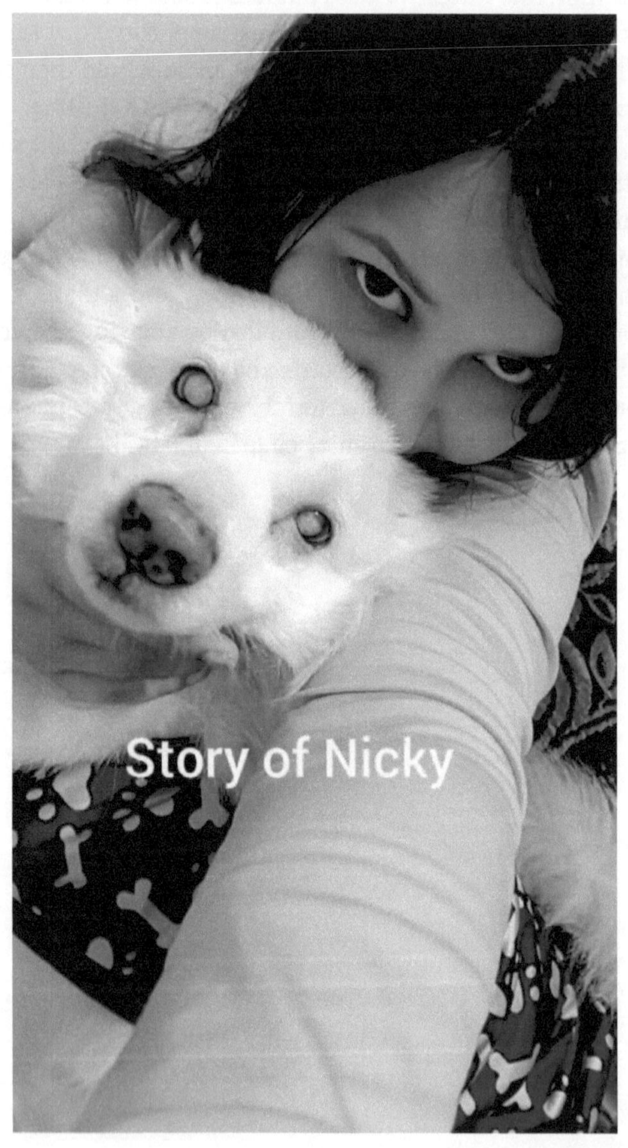

greatest bond ever

Thank you for reading my journey.

www.ingramcontent.com/pod-product-compliance
Lightning Source LLC
Chambersburg PA
CBHW031517150726
47990CB00007B/3062